The Ugly Duckling

Story by Teresa Heapy
Illustrated by Adam Record

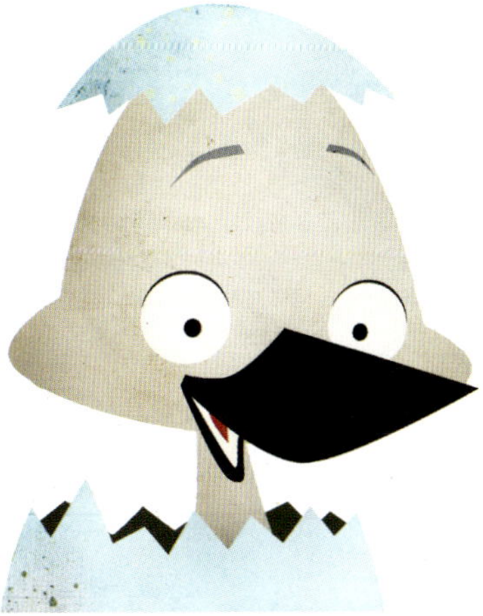

OXFORD
UNIVERSITY PRESS

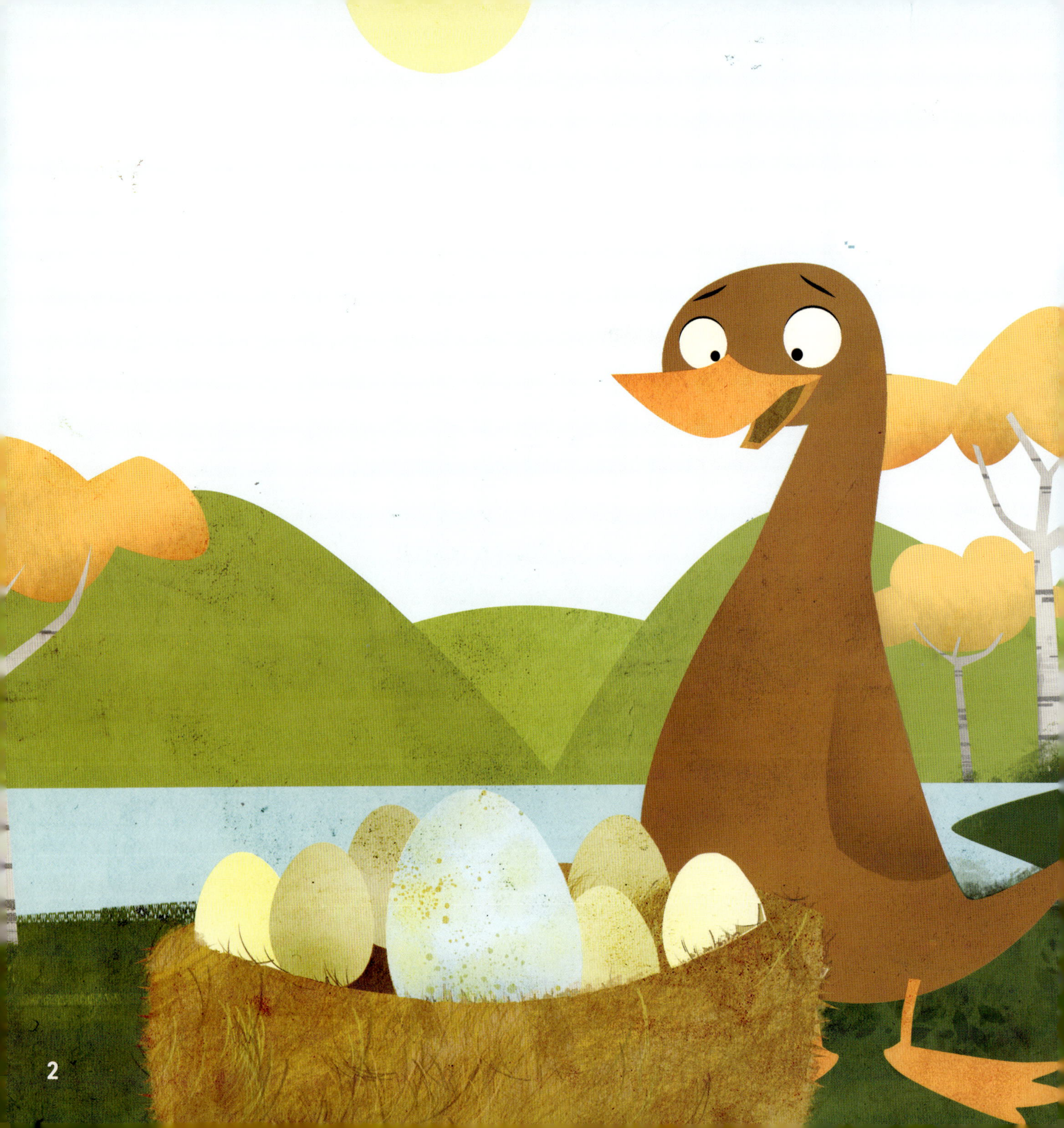

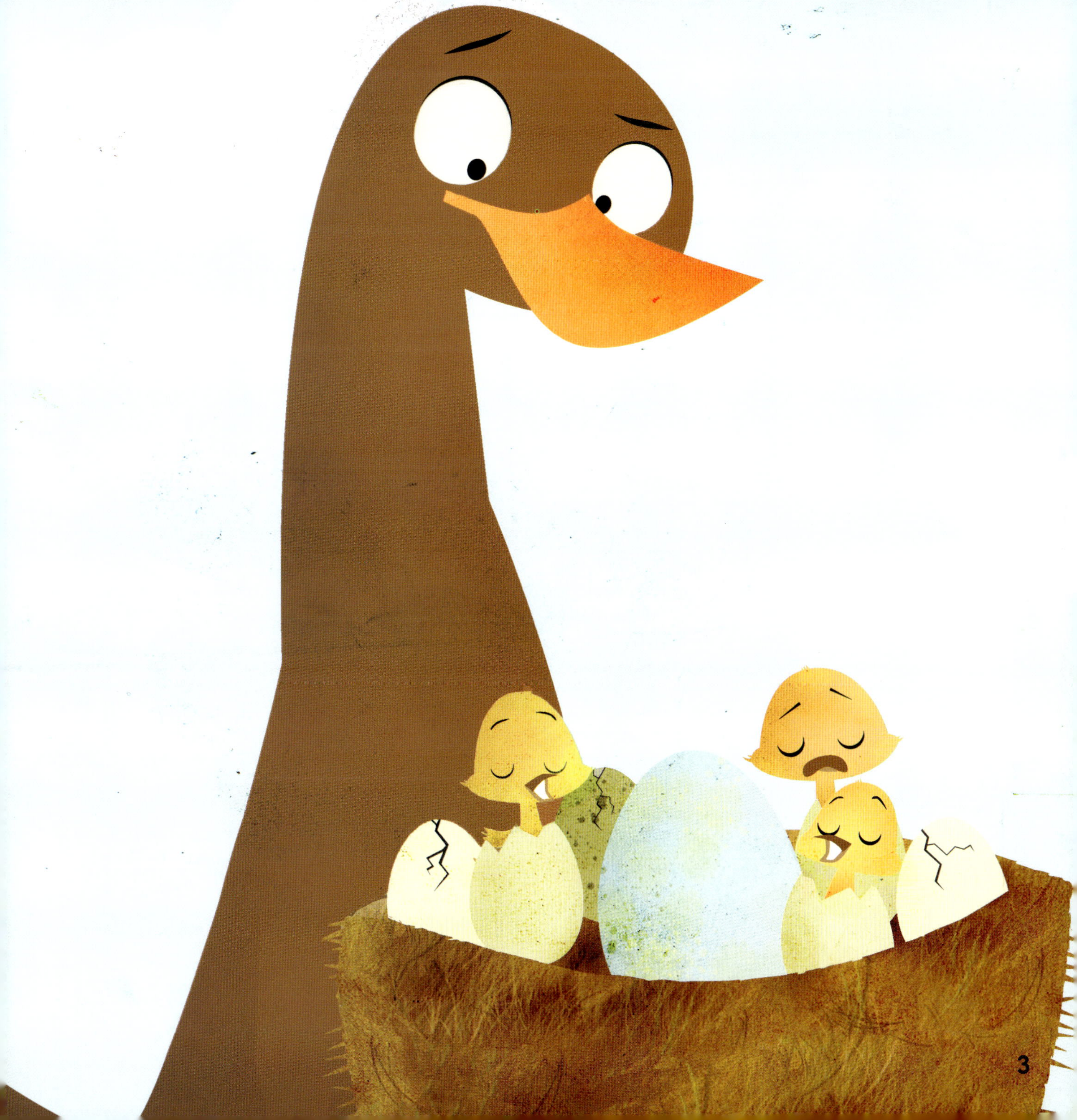

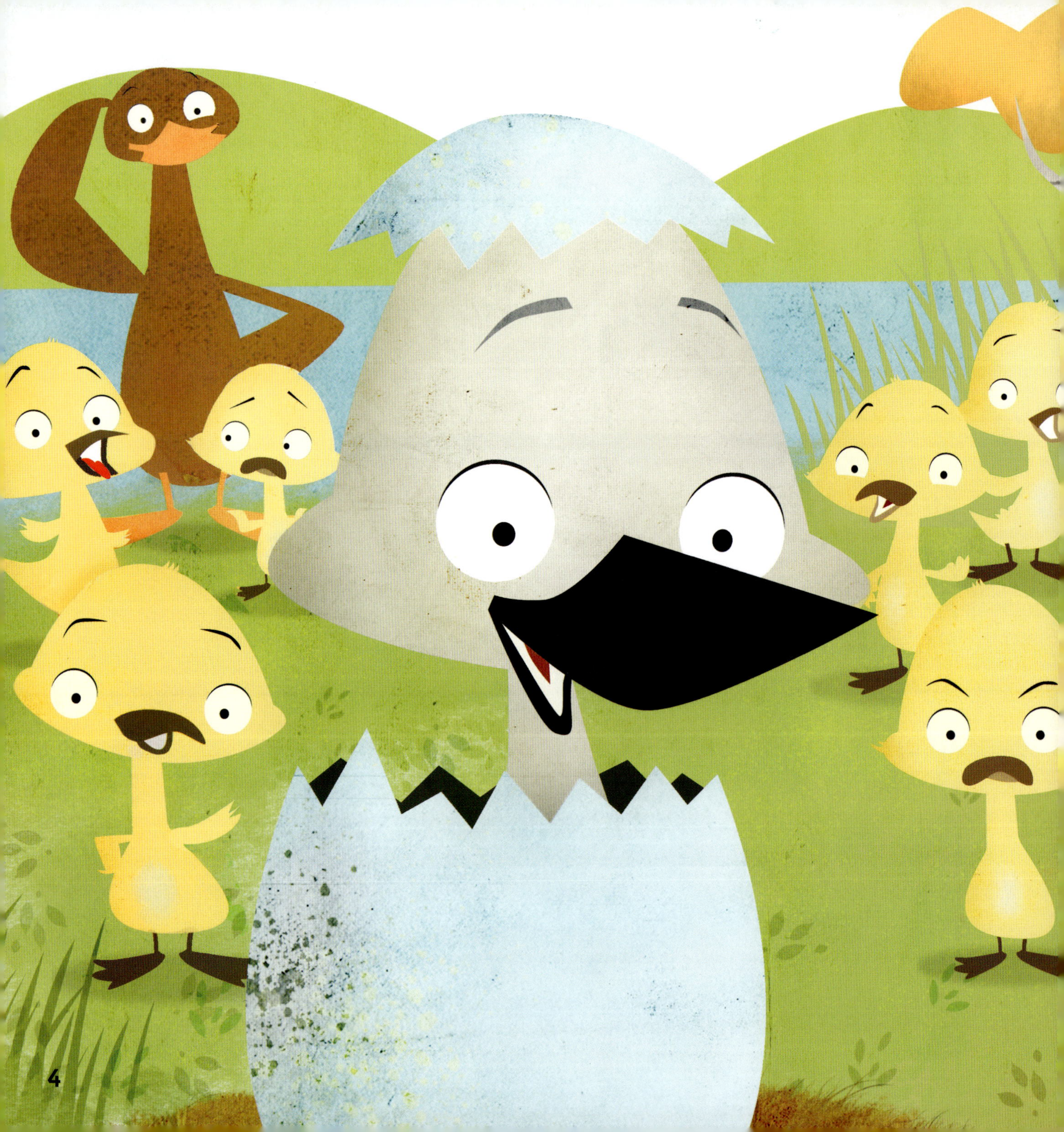

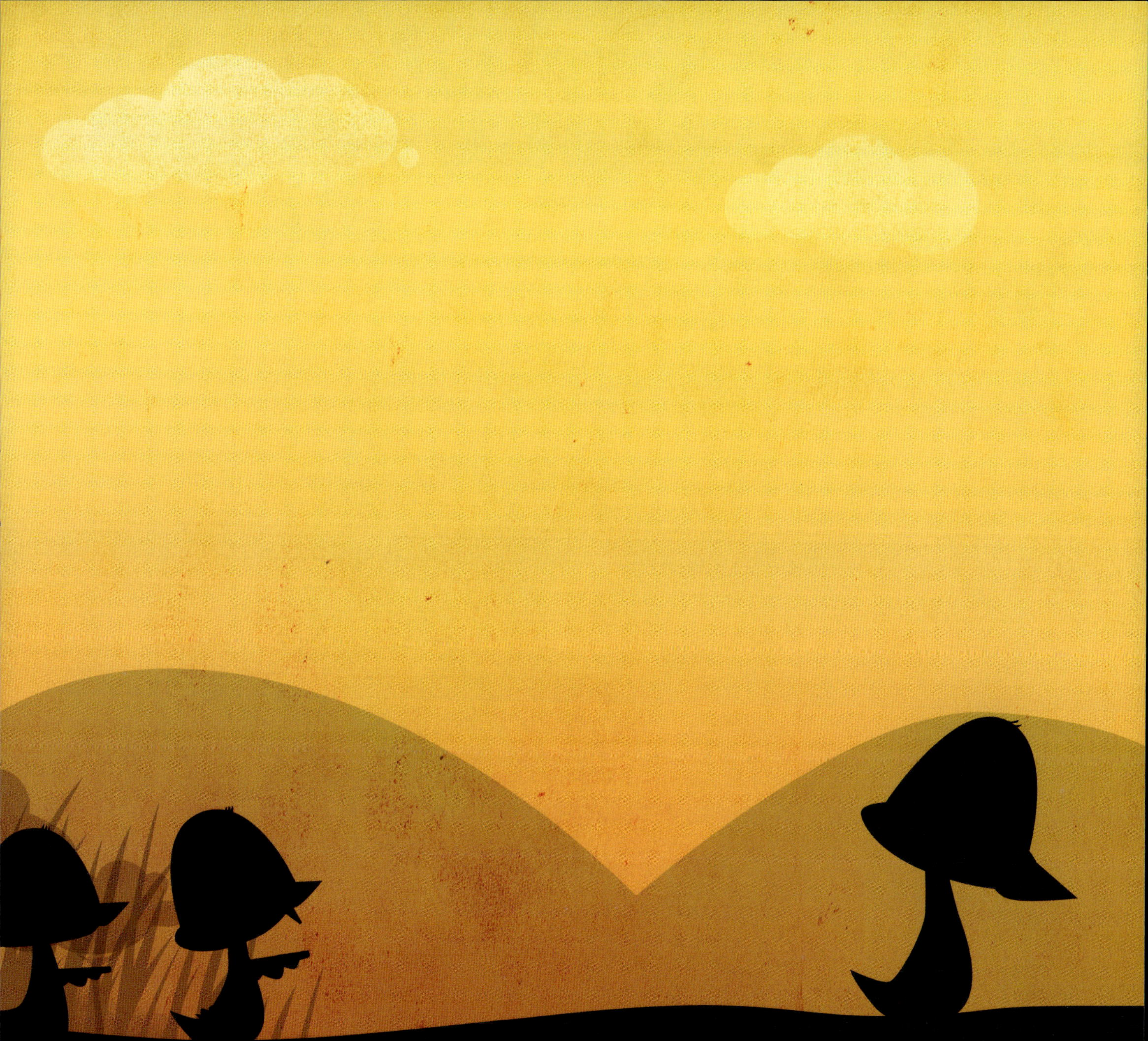

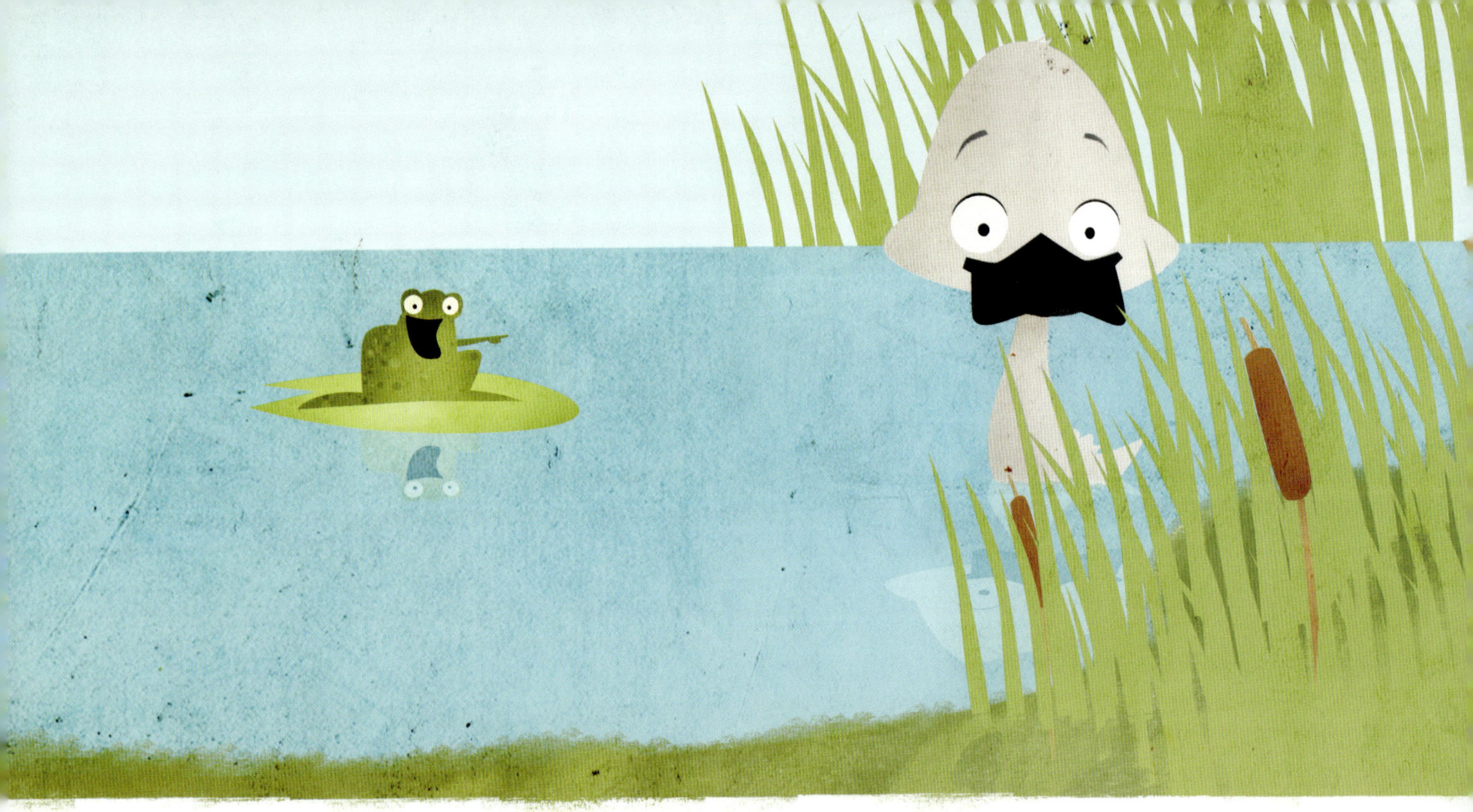

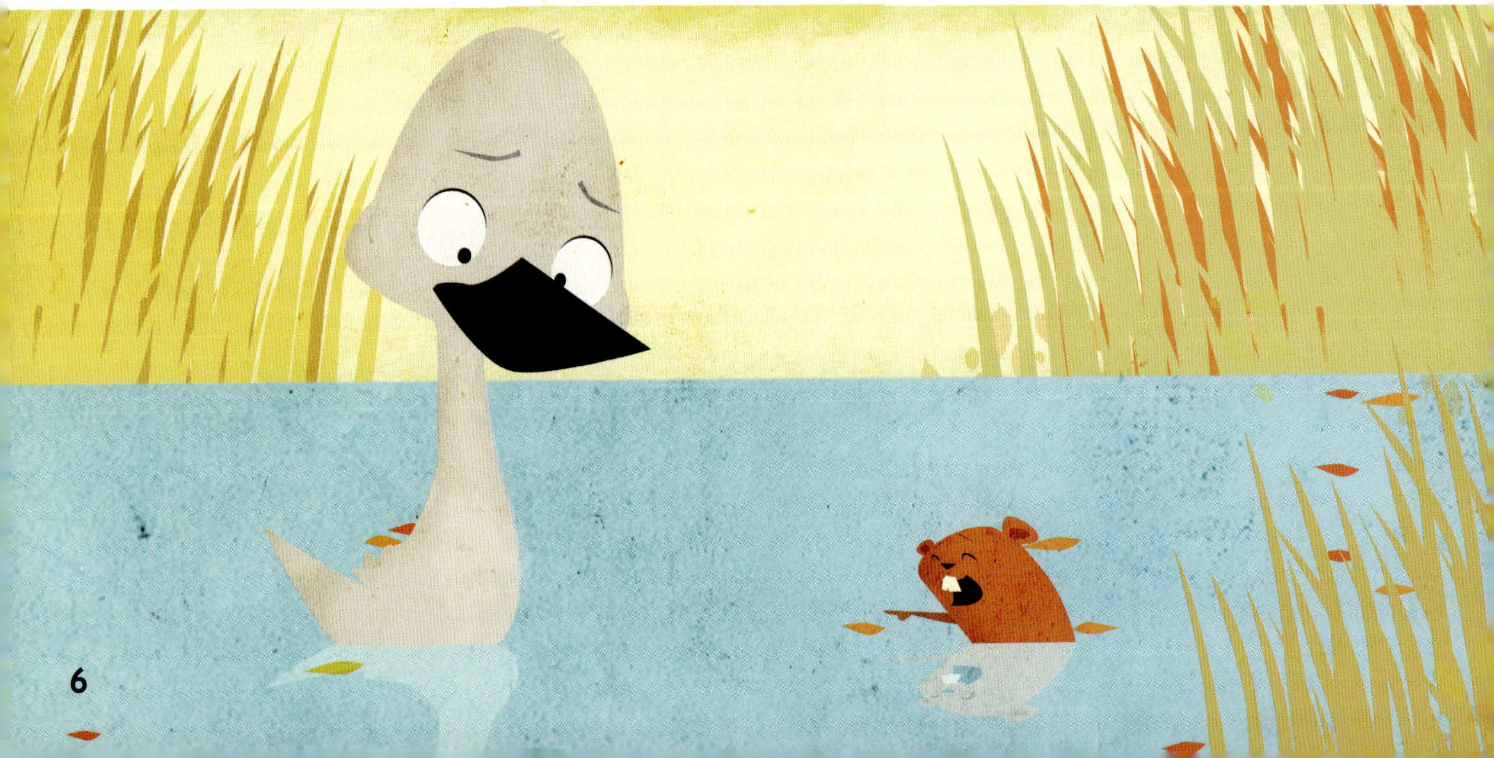

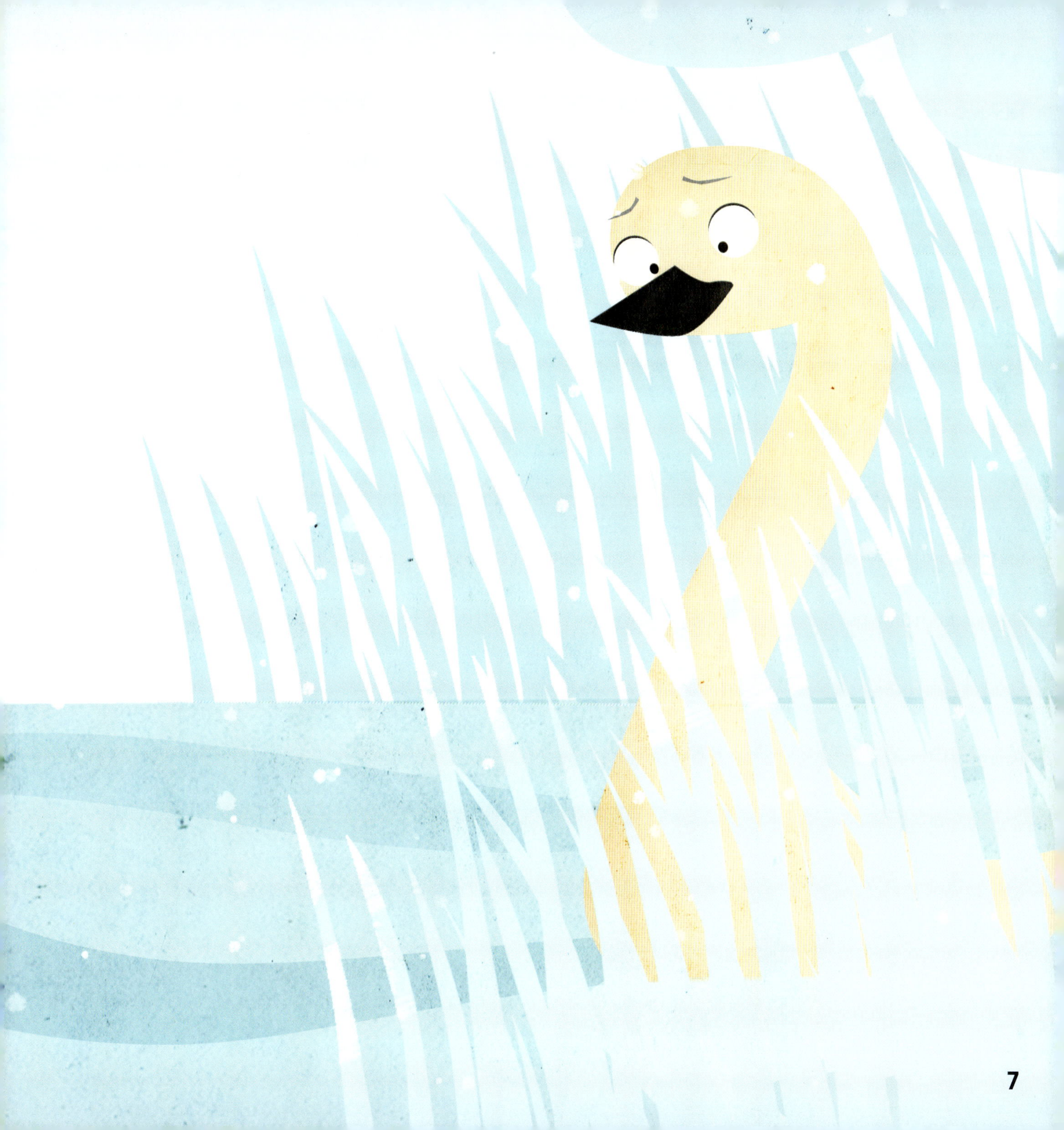

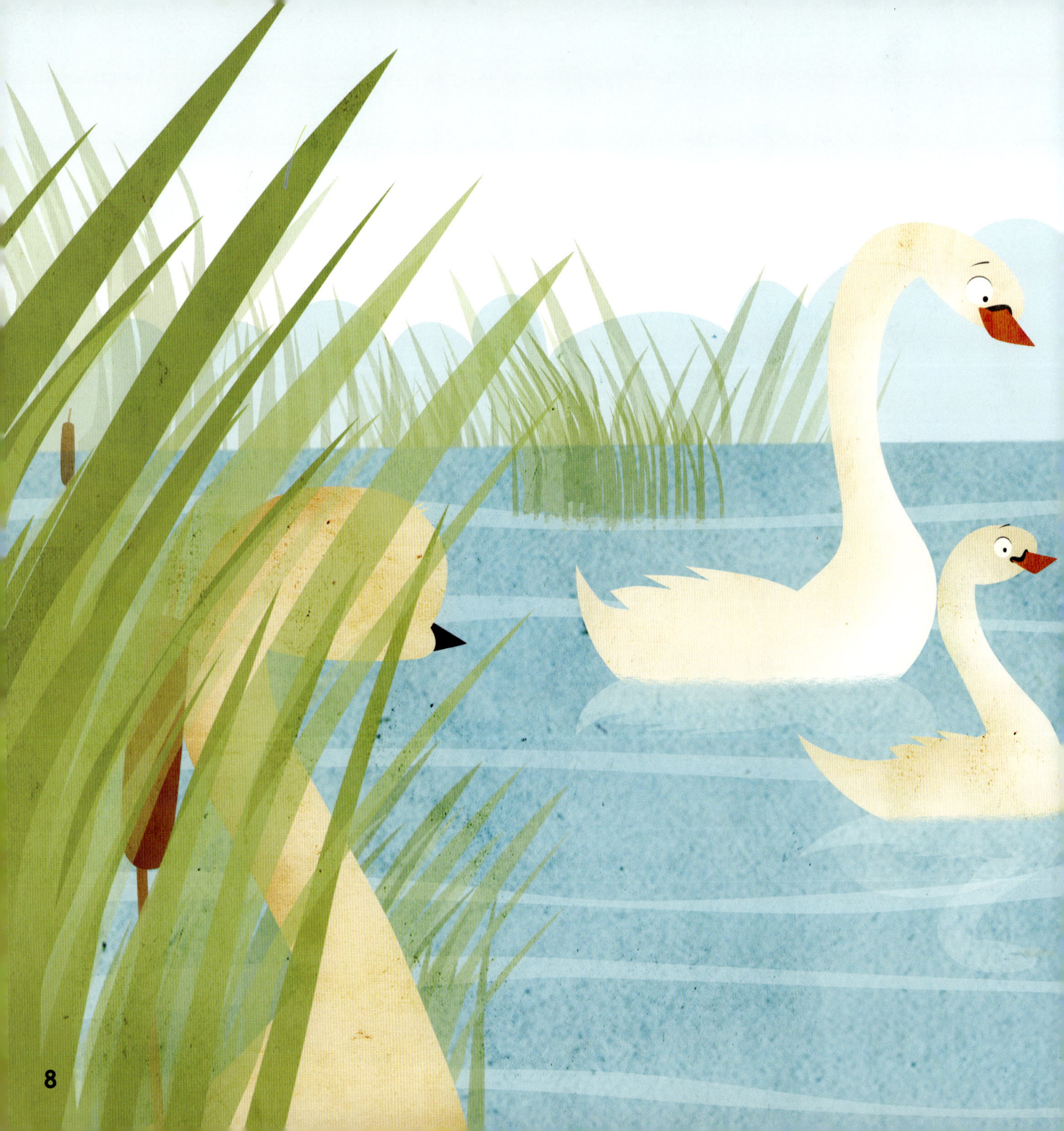

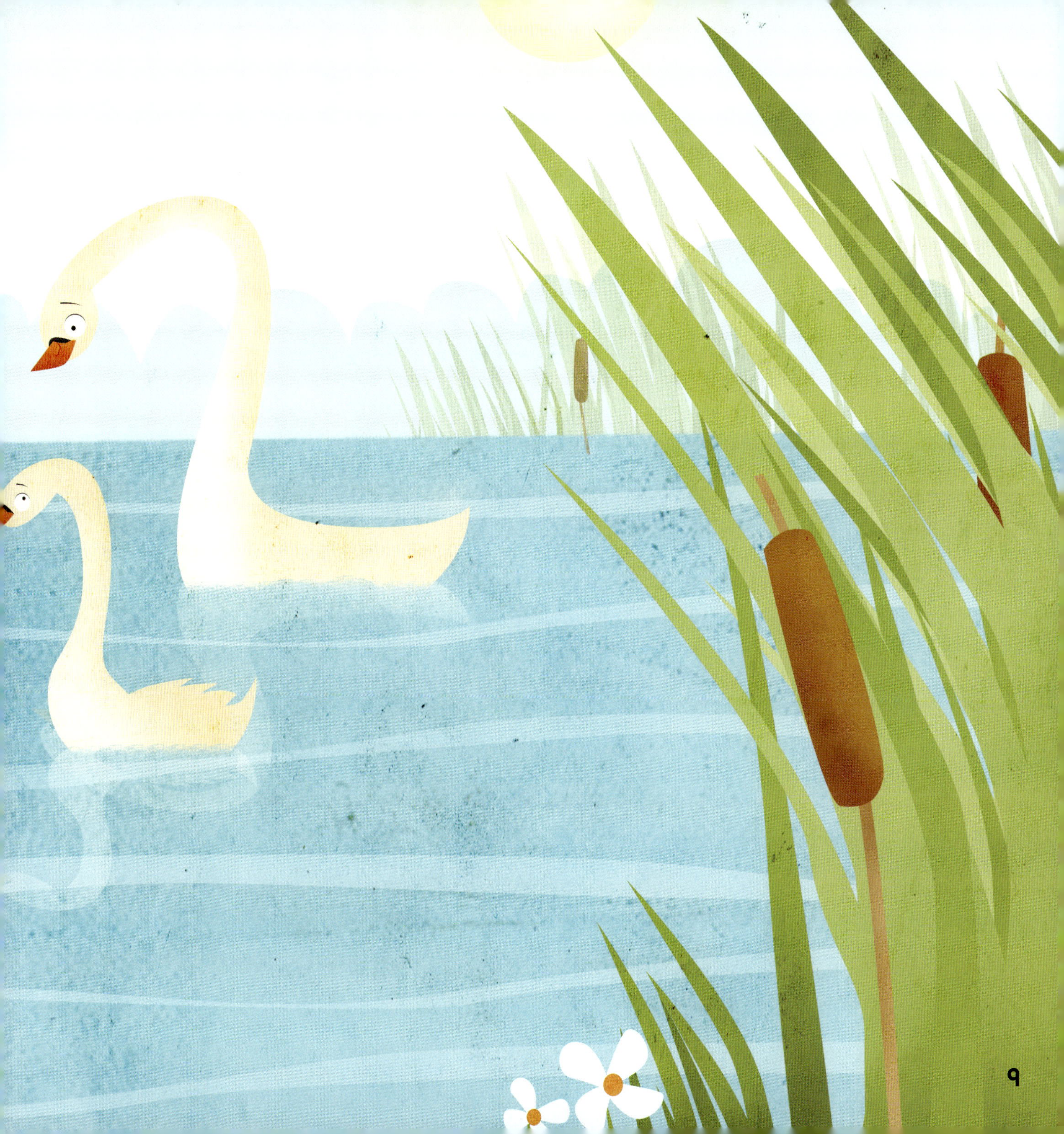

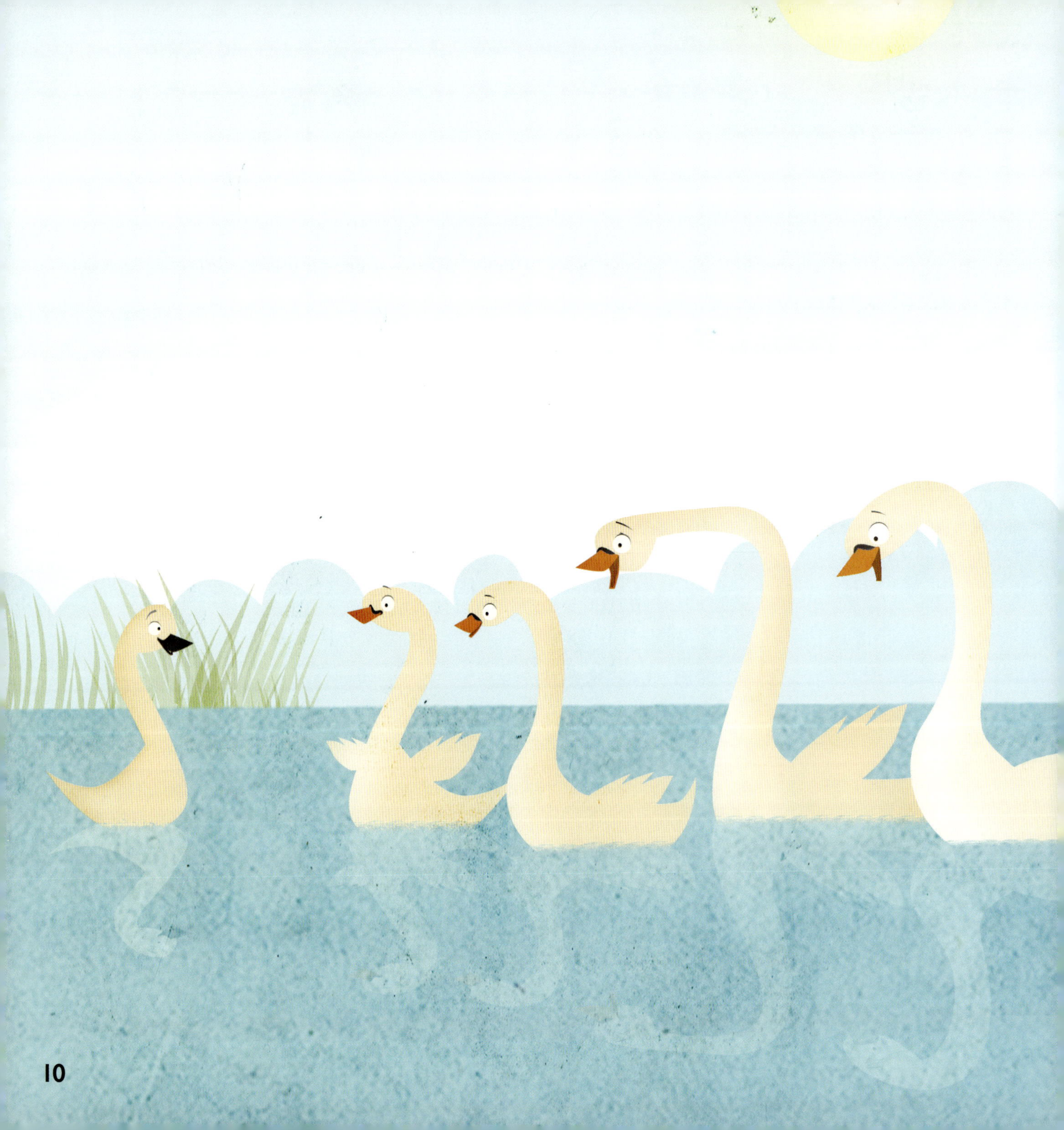

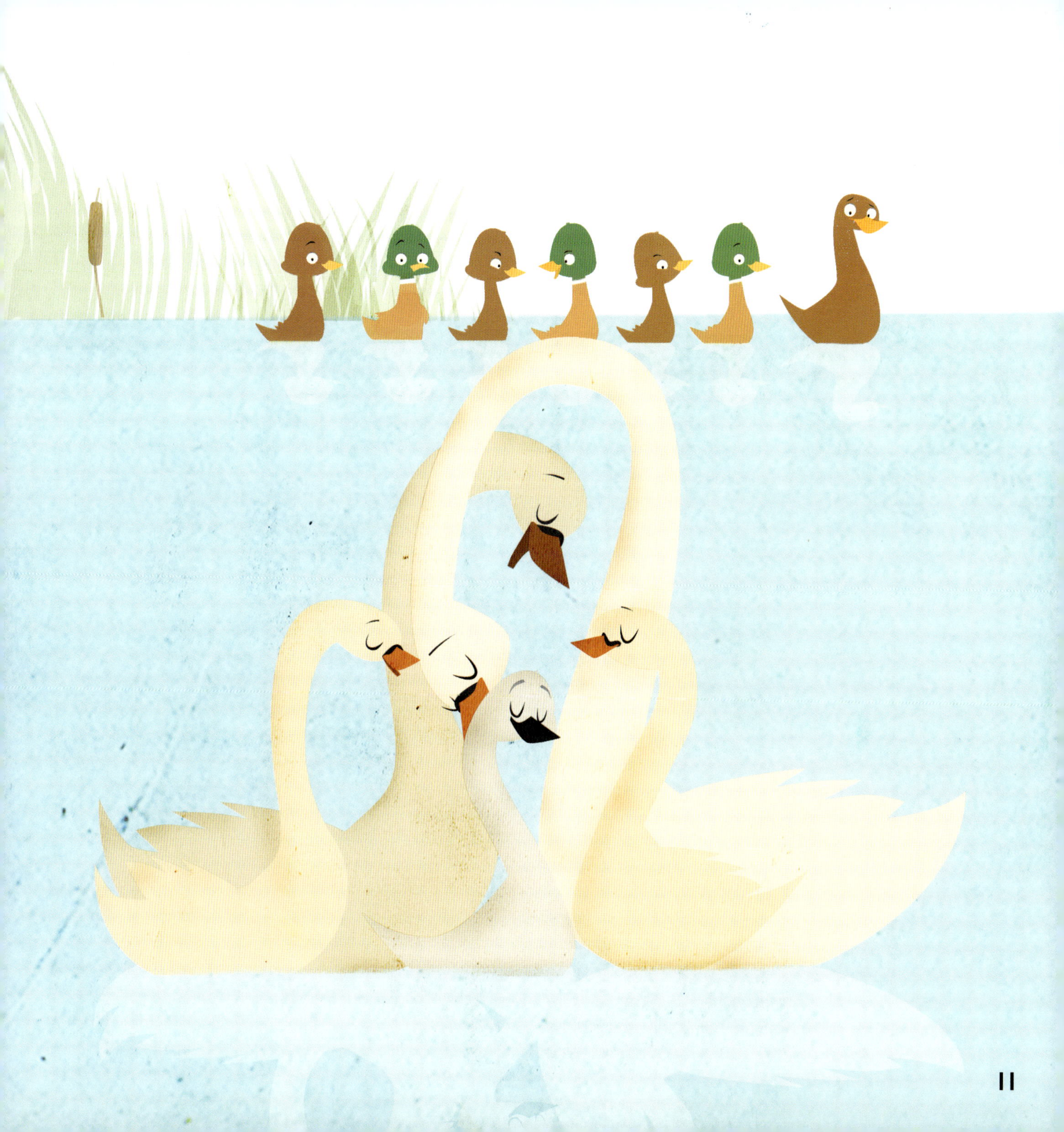

Retell the story

Once upon a time...

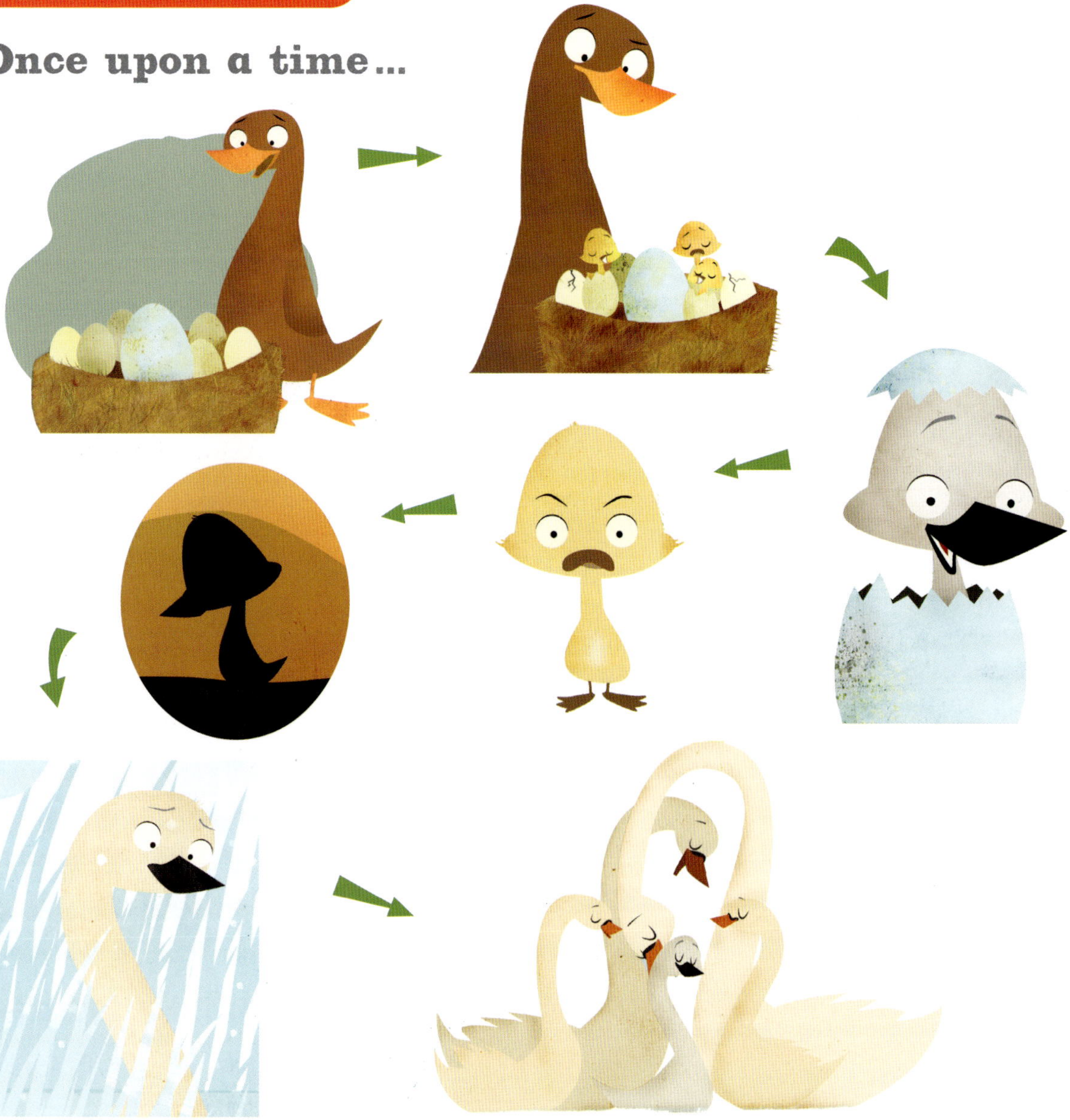

The end.